AF577358

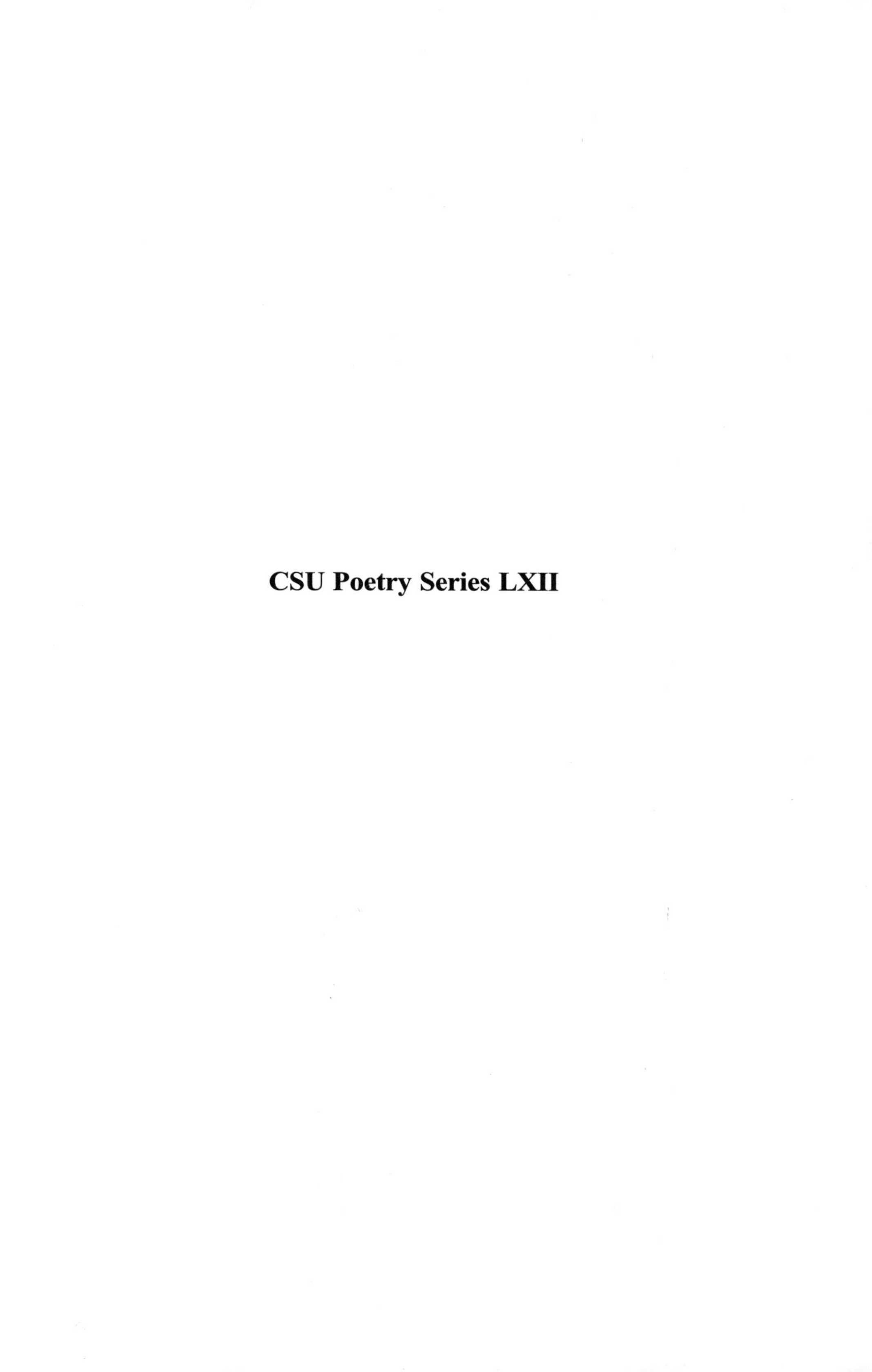

CSU Poetry Series LXII

Double Exposure

Sarah Kennedy

for Julia —
who emerged with me —
21 March 2003
UVa

Cleveland State University Poetry Center

Acknowledgments

Thanks to the editors of the following publications, in which some of these poems first appeared:

Caffeine Destiny: "The Pilot," "Second Story," "The Vandals"
Cold Mountain Review: "Pool"
Common Ground Review: "The Moon and Venus"
Common Wealth: Contemporary Poets of Virginia: "Sin"
Connecticut Review: "Nursery"
Elixir: "Stone," "Girls are Harder," "How My Mother-in-Law Instructed Me in Slaughter"
Flyway: "Relative"
Kalliope: "Visitation Rites"
Nebraska Review: "Shame"
Pandora: "The Starving Girl"
Prairie Schooner: "Pomegranate," "Maid"
Terra Incognita: "Morning, with Tea"

Manufactured in the United States of America

Published by Cleveland State University Poetry Center
2121 Euclid Avenue
Cleveland, OH 44115-2214

ISBN: 1-880834-59-6
Library of Congress Catalog
Card Number: 2002114909

The Ohio Arts Council helped fund this program with state tax dollars to encourage economic growth, educational excellence and cultural enrichment for all Ohioans.

Double Exposure

Contents

I. The Pilot
Felicity 3
Nativity 5
Sin 6
Pool 7
Thief 8
Repentance 9
Maid 11
Kite 12
Bussing, 1971 13
The Good Girl 15
Girl Talk, 1973 16
Blame 17
Church Camp, Southern Indiana, 1974 19
The Starving Girl 20
Whatever You Say 21
Twilight, 1975 22
The Pilot 23

II. Double Exposure
How My Mother-in-Law Instructed Me in Slaughter 27
Dog: 1990 28
Shame 29
Club 30
Custody 32
Looking over Mankato County, My Mind Divided 34
Box 36
The Moon and Venus 38
Morning, With Tea 39
Pomegranate 41
Double Exposure 42
Disappearing Woman 44

III. Arbitrary Specific

Burial 49
Arbitrary Specific 51
Visitation Rites 53
Relative 56
Second Story 58
Girls are Harder 60
Stone 62
Tenant 63
Attack 64
Women's Work 65
On the Freeway 67
City in Fall 68
Nursery 70
Higher Education 71
The Vandals 73

For Rod

I

The Pilot

Felicity

The back lot seemed made for our pleasure alone,
and we dashed our bodies across it, squeezing

through knots of marble-collectors, leaping across
the hop-scotchers. We were sure, Felicity Bonner

and I, we were free in 1968, smart kids in a city
deep in the quiet heartland, though when the kickball

boys froze for the crackling school intercom,
I paused, too, hoping it wasn't another Kennedy

dead, another time for David Hollingsworth, poised
at the corner of 57th and Delaware, to yank my hair

and sneer *Hey, half-dollar*. But she took off through
the diamond's core, knowing I would follow her

anywhere. Such bliss in the chase, I didn't see
who chucked the ball. Just Felicity, hitting asphalt.

She stayed still and, kneeling, I laughed, believing
she was coiled for a surprise, ready to spring

up, jubilant, until I rolled one shoulder back
and saw the blood unspool from her open lips.

Big hands lifted me, hoisted her away,
into the building, and, no, she didn't die, but lay

unconscious for days. Returning, careful
with her clutch-bag of strange pills, she was happy

just to jump the limp rope I turned in a dolorous hand,
around and around, safe from *that kind of play*,

the high school boys were always warning,
will get you into trouble, girls, watch out.

Nativity

How could I wait? Knowing the secret
lay in their room, *under our bed,* my father said,

if you want to ruin your surprise. I cooled
my desire in the yard, skating the brick patio's

skim of ice. Soon, I would get pajamas
or a pair of red tights, for one day Dad

wouldn't leap from the couch to punch someone,
wouldn't stomp away from the mess: *Everything here*

has been ruined by kids. But the dim warm room,
with its curtains always drawn, smelled musky,

foreign. Children allowed in only to place
folded clothes on the dresser or to wake him—

gently, gently—from a nap. Once, my hand drifted
through their drawers, turning her garters, the shiny

packets, and the case concealing the little rubber
hat. My fingers felt it, even after I shoved

the chest shut and ran outside to breathe
moist air, the way I breathed every December, hoping

for snow, some sign the dark month was almost
at an end, and I would sit beneath the glittering tree,

my father passing out gifts, oldest to youngest—
Have you been good this year?—damp with fear

that he'd draw the box away from me, longing
to shred that blossom of ribbon, that foil.

Sin

The broomstick struck soft skin
and my breath caught with pleasure,
but my sister's cry startled me to tear
the pillowcase from my eyes. Doubled

over, she clutched her face. I'd thrust
hard instead of swinging a gentle arc
around the basement—a version
of blindman's buff forbidden by our father,

sure we'd break a bone or the ceiling lights.
But sick of pokes in my back, I'd jabbed
at her laughter. Smaller, I didn't expect
to win, and I knew what was coming

when she rose, angry eye already swollen
and bloodshot. Dad saved me that time,
bellowing our names, and, sudden allies yelling
Molly fell, we tore upstairs. Old news

to our parents by dinner, the red dot
in my sister's gaze fell on me all evening.
For days, I stayed in our father's sight,
prayed as I should, but the bruise refused

to fade until I swept her room immaculate,
even beyond the clean of Dad's white glove.
I plotted my next move while she pointed to specks,
elbowing me to show where I'd missed a spot.

Pool

Molly screamed again, and I fought my way
to the six-foot, deep enough for a dead-man's
float to block my ears when he yelled *Swim,*

god damn it, and flung her loose. She was supposed
to have learned last summer while I dog-paddled
the kids' pool, but she still clung to his shoulder,

shivering *No*, until he forced her face underwater.
My mother, silent behind a whodunit, didn't move.
The older girls, who'd taken their strokes in turn,

sunbathed in a tidy row, strange new breasts
pressed flat inside their suits, but I, always
out of order, flipped to my back and drifted

along the concrete wall, all the way to the deep end
while Molly flailed away. Dozing in the ten-foot
when knuckles rapped my head, I jerked awake.

Donna, the favorite, snarled above me, *What
are you doing down here?* My cracked skull
ached and her nails raked my scalp. Thinking

she'd yank me up by the hair and snitch, I yelped
Look, I can butterfly. I must have believed
it, since I propped an elbow against the edge,

thrashed myself out of her grip, and dove.

Thief

Indianapolis, 1969

Kim slid her thin hand under the glass case
to lift three rings before the salesgirl turned
back with the belt I decided against. Not

expensive, sterling, one with a chip of turquoise,
but they were fast in her fist, and we dawdled
at the door, fingering scarves. *Not this one,*

not that one. The way my older sister might have
talked before she was dragged home one afternoon,
beaten so hard by our dad we all cowered

in our rooms, not even whispering *shoplifting.*
We eased bracelets and tie-dyed T-shirts
from the headshop's open bins under floppy

tank tops and anchored them in our waistbands.
Why not? we sang down the alleys behind
the stores. My father reappearing from cornfields—

They'll never notice this gone—on summer drives
home from our grandparents' farm. My sister, crawling
the hall to our brother's room, where he kept

his paper-route money: *Don't say stealing,*
we call it liberating *now.* I loved the sweet kernels,
the makeup our mother wouldn't let us have,

bought with our pilfered change. Safe
in Kim's room, we spilled our goods to her bed,
deciding what we'd wear to school come Monday,

when all the girls would surround us, jangle
our arms, and sigh, we had such great things,
we looked so grown up.

Repentance

How often had I bent for the blow,
then signed the board my father held?
All I could do was submit in the name

of my own good, of discipline, a father-
hood as distant as the one my sisters
knelt to take inside their mouths at St. Joan's

altar. Every final day of the month,
he drew the broad oak tongue, scrawled in all
six children's hands, from the buffet

drawer and held it to each face: *How
many times do you show up here?*
The older girls counted themselves off

like rosary beads, confessing the sins of a dirty
room or refusing to smile for the spoon of cod-liver
oil, jammed down our throats before dinner.

Rotten to the core, he said, embarrassed
to call us his, and I knew we must be evil,
since our mother, who healed all wounds

with a touch of her Cherokee hands, sat
silent on the sofa, stitching buttons
on his shirt. Then my turn came, and he

pushed the paddle toward me. Dizzy
with shame, I almost dropped to my knees,
desperate to be absolved, clutching the board

where I shone in red, to stop my falling.
I shouted my number, again and again, to keep him

from tossing my names back into the shroud

of table linens, when nothing would be left
but silence between me and him, omniscient
and blood-dark against our white ceiling.

Maid

Clorox bleaching my fingernails lady-white,
from sweet cotton swelling on the sagging line, I
would rush my father's shirts right under

the iron, sizzle them stiff with starch. Only child
allowed to touch his things, I folded perfectly
for his flight bag, my creases at his exact elbow,

my grooves at his belt-line. Even on his weekend
tractor, he'd give over good clothes only to my hand,
beckoning from the door like, I suppose you'd say,

a wife's. But he'd smile, throwing off the expensive
poplin, and for just that I would kneel to shine
his dress shoes as only I knew how, liquid sponged

around the sole, fat wax can and rag. *Either pocket,*
little maid, he'd say, patting at his pants.
Coins in one side, bills in the other. I'd always

choose the hard stuff, knowing two limp dollars
lay in the flat pleat, and when I placed the glossy
black oxfords before him, it stopped my breath

to watch quarters and dimes shimmer down,
the pennies, copper as my hair in summer,
when, oh, he would finally say I looked like him.

Kite

For Prudy

It's nothing, you called, *just run and unreel,*
the thing flies on its own, and it did, red dot

miraculous against summer sky, floating
the way we hovered, midway between air

and cement, in the Y's cold pool. *Keep moving*,
your brother yelled, the one I was half

in love with in grade school, though to say so
would have shamed me. But didn't everything?—

my father kneeling beside me, *Smile now*,
while my sister judged whose teeth were whiter,

then backhanding me for not brushing harder.
(I'd be in the basement later, eating sugar

straight from the bag.) After we flew, I lay awake,
air currents' dip and rise still tugging my arms.

Was that the night I wet your bed, and you sneaked
the sheets to the washer at midnight? I followed,

watching your easy gliding stealth, the way
I studied you the day we laid those pennies

on the track behind your house to flatten
the old man's faces. The train whistled, chugging

toward us along Westfield Road. You arranged
them for their deaths and whispered *Go*.

Bussing, 1971

We opened our eyes at the same time and laughed,
ruining our first kiss but ready to try
again. Scott pushed the bangs from my forehead,
only boy in sixth grade who thought of me

as a girl in a class of, still, mostly white
kids, though now on his side of town.
I'd started the year in my brother's clothes,
no longer needing to measure up

to my sisters' history of beauty. Hauled
in front for the first-day introduction, I slouched,
pixie cut grown out to sloppy layers flopping
over my eyes, jeans so long they dragged

on the floor. Miss Wong did a double-take
at my name, then called it out to snickers
and hoots from the room. What did I care?
Nobody there I knew, the few kids from my

neighborhood who weren't rushed into private
school divvied up among different teachers.
But Scott, one of the students allowed to attend
who lived close enough to walk, stepped behind me

in line to whisper, *Want to visit my treehouse?*
No one noticed we disappeared for lunch
every day that fall, wandering the park, sharing
grapes we swiped from a grocery. By Easter,

we'd explored each other's strange mouths
and started under our clothes, knowing
we'd never exchange numbers or see
a movie together. The last week in May,

our noon hours filled with pinning up art
on bulletin boards for parents who never showed,
I passed him only once in the hall before
the final day, when I was hustled with the other

North-siders onto a bus as fast as teachers
could palm us along. They called above
our heads that we must *hurry, hurry up now*,
since all of us had a very long way to go.

The Good Girl

It was only one spot of blood on my wrist,
but I stared at it anyway, gripping a glass
from dinner so I'd seem to be washing up

if they brought their fight in there. His footstep
on the kitchen floor dropped my fingers
into the water. Finally in junior high, I

only wanted to think about how to sneak
a peek without laughing during a kiss. Then
he was right behind me. I was just clearing

the table—stupid, to step into view
at my brother's *Liar, you said I could*
keep my hair long. I hadn't even sucked

a breath before Dad swung, and John's blood
spattered the living room walls. Mom's black eyes
were fixed on Archie Bunker, and I thought

he wouldn't notice my retreat, but he cleared
his throat, *Sorry you had to see that.* I couldn't
not turn. My role was to walk into his arms,

good girl, while he comforted himself for the muddle
of Indian blood, every one of us ready
to go wild any second. But I was in the middle

of family work. What did I have to fear?
He popped a beer, stabbed a bubble of froth
with his finger. Those days, I was still his *horse*

that would follow the carrot. I raised my hands,
fresh from the suds, to show him, my red
skin blazing through the foamy soap.

Girl Talk, 1973

Jeff and Kay, Ann taunted at the wedding
rehearsal, and I stuck out a lip: *Kay*
and Jeff. Nobody needed us yet,

and our parents shooed us from the sanctuary,
but that was OK, we both meant to sneak
to the garden out back anyway to smoke

and try out our private bottle of wine under
blue Mary's watchful eyes. *Will you*
ever get married? she asked, and I was sure

I never would, but she wanted children,
a boy and a girl, and after we drank a while
and I heard her plan of a perfect home life—

like something you'd see on TV—I wanted one,
too. We were almost family, after all,
my sister was going to take her brother's

name, we were practically twins. Back
inside Immaculate Heart, we giggled
and fell on the pews. *Jeff and Kay!* Ann

whispered. *Kay and Jeff!* I shot back. My
father, adjusting lilies in the aisle, studying
the altar, murmured *Jeff and Kay is correct.*

Ann laughed, but he'd wandered, by then,
to the front of the church, leaving us
to our silly talk. I went sulky, but she

didn't care, she'd already flipped a Bible
open, raising her nose for *In the Beginning,*
the way everyone did with the Word.

Blame

I could have killed her. Streaks of red marker
down the back of my best white blouse: Susie Padgett,
that skinny girl from the trailer court. Who else?

My earlobe still ached where she'd grabbed
my new gold hoop as we stepped from the bus—
Sor-ry!—and twisting to the bathroom mirror

I remembered something grazing my back
between classes. I didn't think anything
of the laughter until Becky swiveled me

by a shoulder in math, *What happened*
to your clothes? My mother would counsel,
Just turn her in. A fight never gets you anywhere.

City kid in a country school, I didn't believe it,
but who knew who her buddies might be among
the girls in leather who smoked across the street?

Staring ahead, I hugged my books when they
bumped me in the hall. Was it my fault
my father had bought that piece of land?

Had I even met the family in that tarpaper house
he tore down? Well, yes, one time last spring,
when the daughter with the shriveled leg told

my parents they'd be out by June. *What trash*
lets a child get polio? my father said in the car,
but I couldn't have known she was Susie's friend.

How was I to blame? My dad was the bigot,
not me, I whined to my homeroom teacher

who scrounged in the Lost and Found for a substitute

shirt. By Christmas it was over, Susie
dropping out, screaming that last day
she hated us all, even the boy whose baby

she carried. Then she was gone, though once
that winter I spied her, lounging in a booth
at the Fifth Street diner, cigarette propped

on her big belly, watching as I ordered
a diet soda. But I was safe. I could forget her.
I may have even turned, in the cold blast

that swept around me on the threshold, and waved.

Church Camp, Southern Indiana, 1974

Bobby's fingers sneaked up my shirt
during *Amazing Grace*, while I swayed
and sang like a born-again girl. Other

couples had crawled to the bushes,
but the camp-leaders smiled and waved
marshmallows while the stringy guy

tuned his guitar for *Kum Ba Yah*. Fumbling
at my bra-strap, he eased me back, and soon
it was time for bed, boys in one building, girls

in another. Next morning he refused to look
my way, but he didn't leave me any more alone
than their Protestant Father or my parents

who renounced our Immaculate Heart
and dumped me there. Communion was Wonder
Bread ripped with our hands, fellowship a gang

of girls around Martinsville Wanda, showing
off her birthmark, *That's where I rubbed on
the cook and it didn't wash off.* My God was still

naked sky-gazing Jesus, arms smack against
the cross, upraised like Steve the youngest minister
conducting the choir. He talked me

into the pool by promising the end was near.
Forgetting early christening, I let him lay me
in the water, where I stared at the sun and waited

for the heat in my breast that would mean
the Holy Ghost's presence, until his cold palm
covered my face and pressed me down.

The Starving Girl

In the mirror, she examines
herself: fourteen and fat, fat
on her hips, her thighs, her breasts
(her father reminds her to hide

them). Skipping breakfast, first
(too busy dressing for school), at lunch
she's ravenous, stuffing herself
and when she gets home, oh, she's fat.

Now coffee and cigarettes fill up
the noon hour, now she can go
from sunrise to late afternoon with only
a bit of cream to cut the bitterness.

But her mother leaves food everywhere,
in the cupboard, the fridge, everywhere, why
does she spread out so much? Dinner
looks greasy and overcooked, roasts

are repulsive, vegetables a waste of time.
Walks after dark allow her to smoke,
she switches to dope, so she can't feel
her legs' flesh rubbing, pushing. She lies

awake at night, stroking her ribs,
her sunken stomach, hearing her own
rapid heart beat, she holds her hands
over its fluttering, she has been starving

for this kind of love, this tiny bundle
of picture-perfect self, light
as the feathers of a swallow,
caught in her thin, sharp nails.

Whatever You Say

Up and At 'Em. Be Part
of the Answer, Not Part
of the Problem. Everything

in *this* house is *Going to Hell*
in a Handbasket, even the car, you know
because every time your sisters move

toward the door, it's *Don't Bend the Rambler!*
And *Whatever* he says, *Goes.* Who
can be fourteen here? Not you, *You'll Run Off*

with the First One-Eyed Cripple Who Comes
Limping Down the Road. You know
you need to *Straighten Up and Fly Right,* girl;

with your fistful of A's, your shiny violin,
you could be *The Donkey That Pulls*
the Whole Cart, but you're stepping into the glossy

convertible of the first man who invites you.
Who cares who he is? He's old enough to know you
Better Than You Know Yourself.

Twilight, 1975

In this light, he looks like the dad who missed work
my third-grade year, when I lay in fever

for weeks. *Best show on tonight*, he says
as cedars stab the last pale yellows and us,

reflected in plate glass, teenage girl and her father
in the new house with the windows facing west—

the direction he once propped me, chest Vapo-rubbed
to a menthol cloud, to watch the sunset

from the porch of our old duplex. My sisters
whisper he cheats on his taxes to have this place

and he's already bloodied a wall
with my brother's nose, but he smiles, and I want him

to linger, the way he stayed beside my bed
until the kettle whistled him away. Soon

he'll be gone again on business, and we
will have a few days to lounge after school,

a morning or two without him tearing the sheets
from our bodies at five a.m. Beside me, he yawns,

Back to the idiot box for you, and I remember
to hate him, though for a second he still hovers,

large in an unlit room, lifting my wobbling head
to let me taste the sweet, amber tea.

The Pilot

His wandering eye, always studying winds
and shifting weather, women moving by:
everything I remember of him flies.

The white tails of uniform shirts, bleaching
on the line, wrapping my face as I yanked
them down, the back of his hand, raised

and shaking, its hard descent.

In flight, he worked the air, surfed the clouds.
Fingers playing the shiny instruments,
he murmured himself toward light. In the back

seat of the Cessna, I, always pulled in the wrong
direction, could only long for the dwindling
fields and depend on him, voluble as a breeze,

to bring me safely back to earth.

But didn't I wish, at least once, when the fist
fell, to see him drop, didn't my sisters all wish it?
We sit instead by the TV whenever a crash is reported;

our mother holds her hand across her mouth. We
picture him in retreat from us and hope
the picture holds: vanishing figure, vanishing plane,

somewhere out there. We think we mean the sky.

II

Double Exposure

How My Mother-in-Law Instructed Me in Slaughter

Brace a broomstick across the neck,
she said, and I pulled until the red head
rolled. The pullet's body sprang loose,

spraying me and the grass, and my hands
found the steaming bucket where I plunged
the carcass up and down until the feathers

loosened. Once, her arm shot past my face
when we arrived for Sunday dinner
to shove a letter at her son from his high-school

flame, but I bit my lip to blood because this
was farm life for sure, eating our own meat,
and though she slammed pans around

her kitchen and hissed, *That blue-eyed bitch*,
when the old man dropped his cane to run
for his girlfriend's daily call, she was showing me

everything I thought I needed to live
in nature. Back then, I told my friends
who went away to school and got regular

jobs that before I would give it up
for the city where my father stored
his money and my sisters, I would just die.

Dog: 1990

Croaked yet? the kids yell, jumping from the car,
but she's still alive, dragging her dead hind legs
toward their voices. *Get back*, they squeal,

guarding their school clothes, but here she comes,
panting with effort, unable to wag the numb tail.
You can't bear what the vet would counsel: *I*

give her a shot for forty bucks or you give her one
for free. The pound would kill her in an hour.
Would anyone believe she crawled into your yard

this way? Hit by a truck, you figure, tossed out
by someone tired of her whining. More practical
than you, with your city-slicker bleeding heart.

Last night, after a foot fell off, your own daughter
laughed from the door, *Pretty soon she'll be*
just a yapping mouth, flopping around, and you

almost slapped her. But why not joke? There's
no hope, your husband claims, so often your children
have already loaded the .22. *Wait*, you cry, lingering

over the notion that those bones might marry right,
given time. But your family knows her life is already over.
They're not afraid to say it. They want action. Now.

Shame

Skull crushed, the Rambouillet flops
in the dust. I drop the box and the UPS man
leaps down, Jesus, he's sorry, he didn't
see. Of course not. The lane cuts through

waist-high timothy where the bucks browse.
Go, I wave. It's no worse than the shorthorn
my husband clipped with the sickle-bar. My mother
has sent a sweater to ease me through the winter.

She'll never visit—I've brought the family down
by marrying poor—so I toss it aside, cursing
pasturing efficiency, the blood of farms, until
my husband storms in, demanding to know who killed

his sheep. *Accident,* I yell, *I've phoned the butcher,*
but he roars he'll file a report. I should be embarrassed
to be so naïve. He slams the door on his way
to fling the ruined ram—*a goddamn shame*—

into a ditch while I cancel my date with the slaughter-house
and, cheeks scalding, call in his claim.
In the morning the driver appears, flushed
almost to tears: why did I pretend it didn't matter?

I didn't know the system, I try, but I've destroyed
his perfect record. *Me?* I sputter, but he
won't answer. I see it in his gaze—white
trash—before he drops his eyes. He knows

I have my rights. *It's not my fault,* I shout,
but, gunning his engine, he can't hear, and I'm glad
his red face disappears in his own tires' dust
when he backs the truck, fast, down my drive.

Club

Things are different now, my sister claims. Only one
of us to marry up, she signs me in as a visitor,

and it's true there's one dark-skinned woman
in the lobby. Three Jewish families, she reminds me,

are here somewhere. Sunscreen-slathered, the old
members aren't that perfect leisure-tan copper anymore,

the way Riviera Club women back in the sixties were,
disappearing through the cedar-lined front gate.

Across the fence, we could hear the laughter, smell
their Joy as we squatted, tossing bread to canal ducks

after chores and before the piano lessons we needed
to grow up genteel. Eight feet of chain-link didn't seem

an obstacle, not as much as the rusty ranges
and fridges reputed to lurk in the channel. We swam

at the Y, anyway, not wanting to make a stink, to be
turned away by the guard. A shame we didn't know

that exclusive meant our parents would have had to change
our name to get us inside. With our new-found political

zeal, we might have stood up to the Rivi kids shouldering
past us at the drugstore candy line, might have held on

to our lanes when they roared past our Schwinns
in their Mustangs. But even now I lie back, pretending

to read until my sister's new sister sighs: she has

a new sitter who's taught her son to say *ain't.*

Now I'll gather my books and huff away.
But she stretches, a lovely arc, and though

I see the belly scar through her wrap, I catch
myself staring like any public-school girl.

Custody

Psychological incest, the counselor says
when I show her the letters, two a day,

my ex mails to our teenage daughter.
It's eight a.m., and I'm alone, thinking

of you. Clutching the papers, I beg
for guidance, but it's a case of arrested

development, she can do nothing
short of a battle in court. Don't I realize

that will do more harm? I don't tell
that the girl yelled, a month before we left,

Get me out of this shitty house. What
was I thinking, following her orders?

That I wanted out myself, but I just cry,
I'm caught between my children. Isn't it true?—

the little one asking now if we'll go back
for her sister. *Don't let your family control you,*

the doctor says, believing it's comfort. She may
be right. My major prof in grad school argues

the same thing when he shows up—just wanting
to help another student/mother—dinner in hand,

a letter of recommendation, new shoes
for my kids' gym requirement. So much advice—

He's not part of this equation, I wailed
to the shrink, though he eased me from bed

last week and held my face. *You're in my*
keeping now, he whispered when I swore

I'd crumble like *that* if my daughter left.
How easily his hands circled my wrists!

And how quickly I called it love—even
after his fingers locked and he looked like

every father I'd known, my pulse hammered
against him, damming my foolish blood.

Looking Over Mankato County, My Mind Divided

Past this balcony, everything goes together;
pale lake, Guernsey herds grazing beside

ripe wheat. Then a crooked seam of fence
stitching the fields snags my mind. Awake

too early in your sister's house, I can't shake
the secret she, unknowing, revealed:

a woman you call precious to others, one
you've told me is just an acquaintance. Blonde,

no doubt. But what's that to me? I've invited
more men into bed than I care to say. You

know it, too, I convince myself, though
plucking a loose hair from my sweater

at dinner, I panicked at the thought you might
notice the color. So I stand, while the lake

turns silver under sun, still telling myself,
though I'm checkered with different bloods—

Irish skin, my Cherokee grandmother's eyes—
I fit into your pure-bred family. One heifer,

neck stretched across taut wires, turns
at a whistle from the barn. The call I learned

on the farm with my first husband forms on my lips,
but I stay silent. Once I believed we could melt

and blend like the angels in Milton's lost heaven,

like the mist unraveling the fence below,

but when I asked which tribe gave this county
its name, you shrugged for answer. I didn't call it

murder, and you didn't say bleeding heart. We
don't fight. Instead, I rise at dawn, pretending

to love the light, while you sleep late. It's easy
to think there's no duplicity in peace, to say

it's all right that Adam and Eve are your ideal,
though gazing over these fields, I find myself wanting

to break into weeping our friends would be shocked
to hear from me, the quiet half of a perfect, civil couple.

Box

Can't you see it? Me stretching out a hand
at the diner—*Let me tell you about the box—*
while he decides on pie? He won't understand,

but twenty years later, who would? Even I
can't believe I married the guy who lured
me to quit high school. When I say, *Just*

the size to curl me inside, it doesn't feel
as crazy as it sounds. *He told people*
he'd built it for tools. Sipping coffee,

my new husband smiles. *He stowed it*
in the back of his truck and I let him
shut me in for hours, never quite conscious,

never quite dropping off. The hostess
by the register flips receipts. My voice
begins to shake. *When he lifted me out,*

I was numb, but I'd follow him
into the house. Shrugging, he asks, *Why*
didn't you call the cops or your mom? Look

at me, squinting through the blinds—
He bought me pearls, called it a game.
At sixteen I thought that was love.

There's no good way out of this story,
not even to mention my brutal father,
the Catholic church, not even to bring up

the old lady at the grocery last week
        who lifted her eyes, then ducked her head, just
as I spied the blue cheekbone. Nobody

wants to hear it. But listen—after
        the wreck, he creaked the camper top open
and fingered the splinters of board. *Look*

how dead you might have been, he said,
        holding my arm. *God means us to be*
together. Before I can speak again,

our waitress steps over, leaving the check.
        Grabbing it, I rise while he fishes for a tip.
You were young, he reasons, *maybe a little*

wild, but I wouldn't make too much
        of it. His expression's flat, closing
down. He doesn't mean to be cruel.

The woman watches him sift through bills.
        She forces a smile. There's a clatter of change.
She's counting the coins as they fall.

The Moon and Venus

Finished with breakfast, he pushes back: *Perfect*
coffee. He sighs. Anything to keep
from saying he is seeing someone else and I
have refused to walk out of my marriage.

A woman tears past us, out the door, and I think
she has spied her husband somewhere
on the street, until she cries out, *Wait, wait,*
I'll move the car! and a metermaid swings

her ticket book closed. I'm relieved for her,
until he comments, *How warm she looks*
in the morning mist! The coffee swirls steam
into the air while he watches the stranger turn

her ignition. I was about to reach across
for our familiar finger-fold, but my hand rises
to signal the waitress. I followed him here,
and it's easy to get turned the wrong way

in this city, but I'll find my office by the skyline.
Lost is mostly attitude, after all, as my father
once said, driving a dirt road after dark,
hours from home. *I know exactly where I am;*

it's everything else that's lost. We hesitate
on the sidewalk, then he grabs my shoulders,
pivoting me, and points to a tiny planet. I know,
from the early news, it's Venus, but

I don't bother to speak, since we're too cold
out here, and it's already fading, delicate
as a dawn-touched bead of water, dropped
from the cup of the crescent moon.

Morning, With Tea

Yellow pine, blue willow cup, broken
loaf of bread. *Still life*, I want to say, my own

hand raised but paused, unwilling
to disturb the frame. Shirtless in this kitchen,

I see again that raging young man, twisting
me to face him, feel myself slammed

into a wall, knocked through a door. The ends
of my hair, as the bathtub filled, trailing

slow wet circles while the shreds of flesh
from his arms soaked out of my nails. Soon

his father's there, a blur of questions,
and me, I'm a naked woman, wandering

off to bed. After the yelling, *My son didn't*
hit you. If my *son had hit you, you'd be dead*,

nothing moves until dawn, Bridget from work
ready to carpool, tiptoeing up the stairs

to find the woman huddled, still, her body
the body I wear. There's no one to call, I left marks.

Have I sat all morning, dulled by ice she's pressed
to my shoulders, waiting for my hand, stopped

over the china cup, refusing to dip the pouch,
to unclench? *Hold it, we're almost through,*

she says, and I hang there while she wraps
my wrist, turns my elbow, and the leaves drop.

It shocks me—my empty fingers, the string
unwinding. The tea, dark against white porcelain,

losing itself, steeping. Such a common thing.
How easily it bleeds under the water's skin.

Pomegranate

Jane licks her hand, bloody with juice,
then breaks the split fruit back to blossom.
What is it this time? You're half an hour late.
Knotting my apron, I rage about my husband

who won't get out of bed because his papers
still aren't graded. *Holed up in his private cave,*
I grouse. Last time, he hired them out to a guy
he paid two bucks more an hour than he offered me

a year ago, when I was his student. *I'll end up*
marking the damn things just to keep peace, hell,
I wrote the exam, too, while he was golfing.
She smears ruby flesh over trout. *Why in the world*

do you stay? When I say, *Queen of Hades,*
she blinks, blank. *Persephone, you know*
the myth? Sighing, *I gotta quit hiring liberal*
arts grads, Jane searches for dill while I ham up

the underworld, arching a thievish hand
toward the marinade. *Do you even* like *this man?*
she demands, slapping my knuckles. I plead
foolishness, launching into my tale of youth,

how he seized me in a weak moment, but she laughs:
It's like what they say about lice. No shame
to get 'em, only to keep 'em. Stuck, I claim
stability for my children (though my daughter

shivers, *Frosty in here*, every time we argue).
She turns to swipe the blade under water, and I
sneak a seed and suck it from my finger, pretending
to pluck at the daisies we cut for our centerpiece.

Double Exposure

Sioux Falls is there, shot after shot of melting
snow, flat highway, him or me,
stiff in front of the froth of the downtown

river. One where I'm waving a mittened
hand at the camera. But an image
of my first husband, kneeling on the roof

of the house we built, slapping rocks against
chimney blocks, shadows each one.
Why not? my new husband sighs,

tossing the prints onto the table, the pictures
I thought would ease this morning's fight. He
accused me, again, of seeing him through the lens

of my first bad marriage. What did I call him—
controlling?—before he shouted, *I'm not
like him,* echoing those arguments

from my twenties when my husband yelled,
I'm not your father. I was about to admit
overreaction when he slipped, calling

me by his second wife's name. We
stared across the room at each other,
unable to rewind the moment before

I cried, *You don't even know who I am.*
It's been a silent day, and this evening
I picked up the photos of our last trip in hope

they would smooth us through dinner. The one

on top shows me smiling, looking like
half of a happy couple. But I'm framed

in something, and, tilting it to the light, I see
the ghost beneath me, posing in front of our door,
the one I slammed in his face the morning I split.

Disappearing Woman

When he grips your waist, refusing
        to let you go *until we have this out,*

you shake your head. But he
        keeps it up, squeezing you breathless,

complaining about your weight.
        Have you stopped eating just to get attention?

You can't even talk—but what's the difference?
        He'll only correct you again, your *groceries*

full of your ancestral *sh*, his insisting
        on the hiss of his single *s*. You could laugh,

remembering your first husband,
        always mad at the way you pronounced

potatoes: too stuck-up for his down-home
        taste in *holler*s and *over-yonder*s. Or

you could whine so he can pull
        you close and whisper *Poor Pal, Poor*

pup, but that routine is stale now,
        so you don't bite this time. Save

your air. Don't reveal you're still
        stewing over the bank statement, addressed

to him alone, nor discuss
        your name, how ill its changed

contour fits, how few times, lately,
        you can stomach watching your own hand

write it. There's no point, anymore,
        in saying that, yes, you're hungry,

in raising your voice,
        though now he lifts you—

look how light you are—
        since nothing of you is left

in this house except your baggy clothes,
        you're practically gone.

III

Arbitrary Specific

Burial

Just thought you'd want to know she died.
My sister's voice on the answering machine,

weeks after our grandmother's gone. No one
went to the funeral, anyway. I can still hear Dad,

laughing after they caught her last year,
speeding away from Satan down the wrong side

of the interstate, and locked her up:
The Wily Indian has struck again. My mother

smiled but left the room. She never said
she was Cherokee. Did she ever say *back home*,

either? *When I was a girl. . .?* Anything more
than *I wore feed sacks to school?* I can't remember

who whispered it: grandmother strapped down,
post-divorce, the electroshock that left her wild

for Christianity. The traveling preacher she dumped
our grandfather for. Some crooked angel

must have grinned above the bed to send her trailing
my father, years later, through our house, waving

plans for her church, *You only have to give me
half your land to be saved.* Easy to stick her

back on the bus to Poplar Bluff, easy to pretend
the Home would take care of her. I don't even know

which man she went by: first husband, second,
her Hoskins father who pulled her mother off

an Oklahoma reservation? *Nobody tells me*
anything, I gripe to my sister later. But I'm the one

who left home, she reminds me, not saying
I'm the drop-out, the one they don't call crazy,

just *a little high-strung*. She believes it helps
when she says that old woman never had a prayer

of knowing any name I might have called. I raise
my voice—*Does she even have a stone?*—but

my sister's got a list of errands to run, can't I
give it a rest? I'm starting to sound unhinged,

she warns, digging up dirt, insisting again
on the story neither one of us, now, can change.

Arbitrary Specific

Doodling leaves in my book while the lecturer
glosses Yeats—*why nine bean rows, why not ten,*

or eight?—I remember the April morning my father
crashed from the roof, landing smack on a broken

length of ice-clotted gutter. Prone on the couch
with a wrenched back that would hobble him for years,

he could still swing a fist when a child walked by.
It didn't matter which one, all guilty of something—

a scratch on the coffee table, a torn book cover,
the carpet stained by blood-spray from a split lip

or nail-stuck foot. That day, a freak spring
blizzard had kept us home, eager for one more go

at the sled while he pounded shingles. After his fall,
all dangerous games were off, and I moped in my room

staring through the window's melting frost. Or did
that storm hit a different year? *Arbitrary specific,*

the speaker now answers herself, *concrete, visual—*
could have been any choice from a limited field,

but I can't stop seeing myself as a kid,
forehead against the cold glass. My favorite sister

waved from the backyard, but the sash was painted
shut and I wouldn't venture past the living room.

I'm sure it happened before we turned his anger

on each other, because she grinned, bent

to the grapevines he'd meant to cut, and I
didn't understand until she disappeared

into the arbor. All I saw were her scarlet
mittens, gently unhooking branches and easing them

down to conceal—or did I hear this story later?—
the wild place we fled to in summer whenever he called.

Visitation Rites

I.
Rose briars tumble down, wild, naked,
almost to the road's shoulder, arching

across each other, dark red in the cold.
I point them out—something to smile at

in the winter we both hate—
searching for an unheated response

to my daughter's chatter about her
eventual children. She wants girls,

girls only, and my throat's tightened,
ready to blurt, *it hurts more when girls*

leave home, though my jaw's clenched.
Ten months gone, phone number changed,

her dad's secretary repeating *he's out*,
letters returned to me by the PO. *Why*

didn't you stay in touch after I moved?
she accused, arriving on the doorstep,

older, thinner, then sat all afternoon
stroking the cat with her foot

while snow settled, flake by flake,
on the window behind her head. Riding

to the mall, she was warmer, of course,
college choices to talk about, the boy

she wants to date, but now
she's stuck on kids; the wiry bushes

are only sprawling bramble, yes
purple, yes pretty, but what a mess,

her father would mow those off, and now
I'm the daughter again, a fifteen-year-old

running from mother to father, not-father,
her father, and I count back years

to my mom's anguished *just-you-wait*,
my clicking the receiver down. I clutch

the wheel and speed toward the parking lot,
screeching into a tight spot—*Sweet,*

she cries—leaving behind the branches, their
chaotic leap-frogging down precipitous hills.

II.
The night has closed around us
by the time we head back

from another evening walk, rules
spelled out before we left—

don't bad-mouth my father;
don't force his life at me.

Cardinals crying *bleaker, bleaker*.
Kicking soft crabapples into bits,

I thought, *The pieces our lives*
split into, coughed a laugh, but said

Nothing, when she demanded,
What's so funny, just pointed to the birds,

little blood-spots in the lindens.
I asked about her grades; she rolled her eyes.

She mentioned her dad's new girl; I didn't respond.
I suggested we stop for a coffee;

she wanted to stop for a coke.
In the corner McDonald's we watched

our reflections grow in the windows
and pretended to see the resemblance.

Now we're returning in silence when a melody,
just four minor flute notes, again

and again, floats from a porch somewhere
ahead. My daughter begins to sing,

and I try to harmonize. We're no good,
we give it up, but turning a corner,

she whispers *Look.* It sounds like the start
of another bad talk, but she gestures ahead,

raising both arms. For the first time, I find it
a beautiful symmetry: limbs, streetlamps

golden through branches, two burning rows
running down the opposite sides of our street.

Relative

Blind from shingles at sixty, she sees well enough
at ninety when I pull my hair loose at the nursing home.
You don't look pretty that way. But I ignore her—*Not*
our real grandmother—knowing I won't keep my promise
to visit more often. Neither does anyone else, not even
my good sister who, back in the eighties (everyone
was separated then), hissed *His first wife died,*
when I mentioned our granddad's divorce. I watch TV
while she remembers dying Queen Anne's lace,
dipping stems into food-colored water, Granddad
teaching us to use the .22 on squirrels. Not me, he didn't,
and, the youngest of ten grandkids, I don't recall
the flowers, though I shrug, *Sure, that was fun*, thinking
how I flew the dirt road toward Milltown, soon as dinner
was done, to the creek behind the pine woods
to chuck rocks at minnows. The time she dragged me,
clutching a hidden barn kitten that had shit
down my chest: *Get on out of this house.* And I got
my legs under me, not stopping until damp needles
sagged beneath my feet. Now she orders me
to fetch the box by the urn in her closet. A rosebud
and a stone. *From our first meal.* She lifts
the rock. *You know what this is? A biscuit I baked*
the day we married. Dropping it into my palm,
she laughs a little. *I'd call that genuine hardtack.*
I smell platters of ham, beans, the pies she taught me
to bake, cracking my knuckles when I tore the crust.
But now she's tearing up. *You know someone was there*
before me. How will we be, all together? Or where
will I be? There's nothing I can tell this old woman

about her heaven. She stares past me, the one eye
drifting behind its cloud. I want to go, but she's waiting
for me to speak, I know she sees the strange, unruly
blood rising in my face, she's reaching right for me.

Second Story

Dirty jeans, overturned cokes, dog-eared books—
    and my step-son, sprawled on his quilt in a white tux,
home early from the high-school prom because

his date went with someone else. Flunked-out college
    kid, too big for the monkey suit, he ripped off
the powder-blue cummerbund and tossed it away.

Down in the kitchen, his dad slammed a cabinet.
    It was the second time she'd stood up his son,
and I meant to slip past and be at the gym

by the time he began the lecture on being a man,
    but I stopped when he wailed *I'm shit*, though
given his arrest for theft, I was inclined

to agree. I wished she'd dump him for keeps.
    Then he was crying into his pillow, big baby,
and it struck me—*Did you two get an abortion?*

Leaping to whisper *Quiet!* he covered my mouth
    with his hand. I'd heard my husband, too,
railing about his last wife, the Down's fetus

she wouldn't bear. Then I got it all:
    the run to Illinois, the mall visit
afterward. *I didn't want her to dwell*

on it. Great. Just like his old man—
    I didn't really hit *her*—after his ex
warned me he cold-cocked her during a quarrel:

She wouldn't shut up. I had to slap her a little.

          I'm years away from all that. What is it about
the scene that grips me still? My arm being

grabbed, the wall below taking a little punch?
          Or is it myself—the way I stood on the landing,
lost in imagining my first husband's face,

how he would have loved to hear of me
          fleeing another marriage? Later, I wasn't afraid
to say they were crazy, to tell stories of rebound's

hidden dangers. But what I left out was me,
          paused with the one looming on his threshold,
just as the foot of the other one hit the first step.

Girls Are Harder

(I)
Their snotty mouths get to you, Ann complains in the faculty
lounge. Last night, her daughter stormed from the house,

the pissy little bitch. Laughter all around, even from me. Hell,
the girl bragged in my class she'd write stories

about her mother, *but not until she's dead.* Ginny, who has only
sons, jumps in, anyway, *I'll want to kill the ones they date,*

the whores. Ann, face flushed, stirs her coffee and I just stare—
her kids are still in grade school—while she rushes on,

*You always know where boys are coming from. A punch
or kick. It hurts, but it's good clean rage*:

(II)
When the raped woman on the film began to enjoy the sex,
the man who'd picked me up outside high school smiled.

Fifteen, my first porn flick, I sat, quiet as my parents taught,
and studied the actress's face. After stopping the reel,

he twisted my wrists, *Let me tie you up, just once*. Does it stretch
the truth to say I was a child, that I wept like a child?

That I begged forgiveness when he turned away and lay down
silent for him? I gazed over his shoulder and got smacked,

that night, by my dad for a sullen face. How politely I sat
during dinner, skin of my cheek stiffening to bruise:

(III)

Darlene, on the phone (her paper is late), breaks into tears:
        mother's *gone Stepford,* father's spent spring tuition

on *some new chick*. Wild girl off her meds to finish finals,
        she's already flown into class, yelling at Stacy, *you snitch,*

you little suck-up, until the poor girl tore from the room.
        Darlene ran, too, and when I sputtered—*what the hell?*—

Tamara laughed, *Females can be nasty*. A little dope in the dorm
        last night and someone e-mailed the dean. She'll improve

back on Paxil, but everyone says don't be soft on the ones like her.
        I steel myself when she starts in on the stepdad,

He hits me, and I swear at him, and then he calls the cops. Mom
        says to be nice, to stop seeing older guys who treat me like dirt—

already I feel myself relenting, though my face burns to think
        of my chairman, smiling, shaking his head at another story

to justify lenient policies. The crying stops, *I wish that fucker*
        would die, and her voice is edgy, tough.

Stone

Will it always be there,
swelling my side? Don't I love
my daughters as all parents

do, waiting by the window,
nose pressed against the glass,
as my mom used to say

of her mother? I fluff cushions,
whip a dinner up. Then one
will remark, their father's so

white-trash, will mention
the unpaid mortgage, the credit cards,
the girl he calls his new best friend

(she's seventeen)—*what*
a loser—then say they'd rather go out,
and it rolls under my breastbone

like the head of a child (not
his, forced into my body,
my face shoved into the pillow).

When they hug me goodbye,
I remember the day, after I found
the will to gather them and go,

when they said they loved only
him, who *needed* them (how
easily, then, he wept), and it bruises

me, under the ribs, just as I,
long dry-eyed, squeeze them,
hard as I can, in my arms.

Tenant

The teacher's gotta be lying, sobbing that a man
broke in. *Ma'am,* they suggest, *maybe it's one*
of your students? Colonial Heights cops:
busy patrolling the boulevard for undergrads
from the Black college—out at night, they gotta be

into something—they're ready, oh yeah, to take
the call. But when they see her pale skin and hear
where she works, they rifle her place—*any drug*
use?—and pocket the money from her purse—
it's evidence. By now the landlord's at the door,

yelling *You can't break your lease,* while they ask,
again, if she'd recognize anyone from a class
if he appeared in her bedroom at night. *Of course,*
she says, but they click off the recorder and walk her
out, each gripping an elbow, to the squad car

waiting to haul her off to Petersburg Hospital
(tucked between propped-up Civil War buildings)
for the regulation rape exam. Hours later, she
feels her way from the room in a strange new body,
and they screech away before signing off on the bill. She

fumes at being forced to pay, but when the attendant checks
her address he shakes his head, *You know we call it*
Colonial Whites?, and taps the exit's rubber mat.
Emergency's doors hiss open to morning in the South.
The old sun floods the parking lot, and she's free to go.

Attack

On the phone after the break-in, he
tells me it wouldn't have happened if I
had called off the divorce. I wouldn't be living

in this seedy apartment, and his simple presence
would have protected me. Still shaken, I
start to cry. He murmurs it's OK, thinking

I'm in nostalgia's grip. He's not angry, no
hard feelings, court can be postponed. But
I'm recalling last night, pressed on my stomach

in bed while the stranger bound my wrists and ran
a gloved hand down my naked flank. I knew
what would follow. *Even at that moment*, I blurt,

reckless now and mad, safe though the back-door
pane lies in fragments, *or when he walked me to the tub*
and said get in, when my only thought was I'm gone

already—Enough, I can't hear any more, he
whispers. I hear a click but still I shout—*even then,*
before I'd've lain back down with you, I'd have

shoved my throat against his knife. The line
is dead but I shake it like he's still inside—
He didn't really harm me, I'm yelling, *he didn't.*

Women's Work

Can't, I managed to squeak (exertion
not to shout) when Adam from History
asked last week if I'd meet him for lunch

to talk a little shop. He'd been reading poems,
he smiled, he wanted the new prof's
opinion. I gestured across my desk, *too busy*

with grading, but his nod said *She's a snob.*
What's my problem? He isn't anything
like the adjunct at my last place, who followed

a chat over cafeteria coffee with a message
on my voice-mail: *I've been dreaming about you*
lying in a pool of blood. He was best friend

to the chairman who summoned me, after
I worked myself up to file a complaint: too bad
the system didn't use a tape, my word against his,

poor guy, not even full-time, did I want to cost a man
his career, maybe it was someone I used to date?
He was *concerned* that I not *damage my position,*

(hand on my arm) but I fled my plush office,
the colonial campus, the unsigned note, typed
on school stationery, *You've made a serious enemy.*

People here are different, I assure myself,
though my finger flickers over *Record*
whenever my phone rings now. It's only Adam,

trying one more time, too polite, already sorry,

he knows I'm swamped. My face, all angles,
is a shadow in my computer screen. My ex

used to swear only homely women cried
harassment. *Anything for male attention*. I want
to end this call, but can I afford to tell the truth?

I yell to a student who isn't here, *Just a second,*
Sandy. I plead job stress, not a minute to spare,
though, even to me, it sounds like a labored lie.

On the Freeway

Double antenna, dammit,
        I tap the brakes but, late
for work, steal up
        the right-hand lane to check
him out. Not watching
        the rearview, maybe not
a cop, just a guy
        with gadgets. White
shirt—uniform? I'm trapped,
        watching the kid
in the back seat
        wiggling a finger
at me. They're not
        talking, there's no wire
cage, but the driver picks up
        a phone, and I drop back, locked
at 70. Of *course,*
        the sun rips a cloud,
I can't find my glasses,
        I'm stuck here blind for God
knows how long. Flash
        from a window, my arm shoots
up. The spark rises too, it's not
        from the car's glass, no
it's sunlight glaring
        off steel on the teenager's wrists.

City in Fall

By early afternoon, the blood is only a bed
of darker earth. Scraped to dirt, the yard no longer
marks a man's shape, nor does the glare

of new window show the bullet-tattered blinds
that still droop behind it. How different
the world this morning: mist coiled into spruces,

trampled grass, glass on the dusty sill
coal-gray when I stepped without a sound
from the front door to find orange tape

blocking the driveway, a cop guarding
the walk. The parking lot hollower
than even last midnight, just before I heard

four shots, then silence, then a fifth.
I lay, wound in sheets, wondering
whether to run for the phone or stay flat.

The lamp in my hall, left on for comfort
since I woke once, months ago, to find a stranger
in the room, would have made me a silhouette.

But soon, lights stained the curtains red and I rose
to see a young man, face-down on the turf below,
gun in his hand, lying in front of the pane

he'd fired into, where a young girl wailed.
Two ambulances sat, one for the wounded, one
for the dead. At dawn, fog shredded

the city while the autumn night bled to day.

My hand, reaching for the news, made the only noise,
skidding against paper, past crimson poison ivy

curled into the impatiens. How can I describe
to you the stillness? The air was stunned,
so cold that my body's imprint stayed

in the bedclothes until, startled by a helicopter
thudding across the sky as I dressed, I shook
the cover out, hard, and snapped it down.

Nursery

Pinching pea-stems curled in her hand,
squeezing a ball of soil until it's veined
from her palm, my sister still bitches
her way through our old neighborhood

school, popular kids chasing her through
the bushes that bordered the playground
of PS 84—*marymoogret, marymoogret*—
her big frame slow in shouldering branches

aside. I spat the only dirt I knew—*protestant*
bastards—and escaped. Same size four years
running, I slid under the fence and was gone
across the street to our Immaculate Heart,

the nuns our father no longer trusted, while she,
pitching fistfuls of mud and leaves, stood
surrounded. Soon, I'd wet the bed again,
and, triumphant, she'd toss the sheet, blooming

with pee-stain, at our mother's feet, *Why*
do I share a bed with her?, while I wept. *All*
the way home, I tell her now, *I despised them*
too, but she still cultivates the glare

she used when she'd catch up to me
at the drugstore on 57th, already sipping
a coke and working math problems, my nails,
on the new white paper, scrubbed Sunday-clean.

Higher Education

When Monique appears in my office door,
long legs sheathed in swanky jeans, I know
what she's after. Now I have to shuffle, fast,

since I never use the gradebook I'm assigned,
just scribble the letters out on whatever's handy.
She's my favorite this semester, smart,

just a little lazy, but her long nails trail
across shirt-tail, then hair, before she offers
a plaintive *Professor?* I want to stop

those tentative fingers: I've been her,
teenage girl peering into mirrors. Teeth
too large, breasts too small, I just wanted

to be looked at. Someone finally did, of course,
a man who studied perfect form: my hair, not blonde,
did not rate at all. My eyes got a five, lacking

the required blue: *You're full of shit up to here*
(edge of his hand chopping face from brain).
Mouth too big, belly a five, back OK, breasts

approaching ten. Years later, ready to leave,
I threw my hands in the air—*Ten breasts!*
I'm an Ephesian Artemis!—but he failed

to see the humor in *that* remark. We were
1 and 2, we were *Adam and Eve*. The day
I turned eighteen I cried, old enough for wrinkles,

while he petted my hair. *Weeping will only*

bring them on, and that will teach you.
Back in school, I complained over every score,

sneaked off with the profs and the boys
with brains. A-men, I knelt at their feet
and took whatever they handed out. Jesus,

that's a long time ago, but here's Monique, adjusting
her bracelet before she unfolds a term paper,
murky with grammar errors. *About this B . . .*

I find the rumpled sheet where she's recorded.
Oh hell, 89, 91, it's as arbitrary as they think.
I trace absences as though they matter, stabbing

down on both of her Xs, but she flinches,
and I have a feeling, if she asks me again,
I'll write in the mark she expects.

The Vandals

Years later, you laugh at our destruction,
two kids on bikes in the sixties stalking billboards
in Indianapolis, pocketknives in hand to shred

advertisements for consumer culture. *Remember*
the creampuffs? How could I forget jamming
five dollars worth apiece in our backpacks,

sliding down department store aisles, sticking
pastry in trouser cuffs? The system was burning
down around us, and we refused to be left out.

Your dad bicycling to work, my mother buying
whole wheat bread: ahead of the other parents,
they couldn't have known their kids would turn

on *them*. We planned further action under
the beat of our sisters' Crosby, Stills, and Nash,
went ignored during the yelling when my dad

smelled pot on my brother's breath. Quiet
on the front porch, guzzling sloe gin in cokes, we
giggled like good girls. They hardly noticed when

we packed our bags for the country. *We never looked*
back, we brag, trading stories about my sister's
new condo, your corporate brother's eighty-dollar ties,

neglecting, for the moment, to mention our
middle-class jobs and houses. *Have you ever told*
your mom how bad we were? you nudge,

but that's the last image my mother and I

need scrawled across our picture of happy
adult reunion: teenage me, wild with delight,

stuffing a twist of monogrammed napkin
under the coals in a woodstove, then
kneeling to blow the family linen to flame.